Raising a *Lady* in *Waiting*

Daughter's Workbook

RAISING A *Lady* IN *Waiting*

DAUGHTER'S WORKBOOK

JACKIE KENDALL

DESTINY IMAGE® PUBLISHERS, INC.
P.O. Box 310, Shippensburg, PA 17257-0310
"Promoting Inspired Lives."

This book and all other Destiny Image, Revival Press, MercyPlace, Fresh Bread, Destiny Image Fiction, and Treasure House books are available at Christian bookstores and distributors worldwide.

For a U.S. bookstore nearest you, call 1-800-722-6774.
For more information on foreign distributors, call 717-532-3040.
Reach us on the Internet: www.destinyimage.com.

ISBN 13 TP: 978-0-7684-0367-1

For Worldwide Distribution, Printed in the U.S.A.
1 2 3 4 5 6 7 8 / 17 16 15 14 13

CONTENTS

A Message to the Daughters

While I want to encourage you to re-read the preface to the book (or read it for the first time, if you have not opened your book yet), a reminder never hurts!

The wonderful thing about going through *Raising a Lady in Waiting* in this format, and what you can expect from me along the journey ahead, is this: authenticity and experience. I know where you've been and I want to encourage you, drawing from my personal history, on how to become a young lady in waiting. To be the young woman who waits for God's Boaz and avoids Bozos like the plague, it is so important that you understand your mom's role as your greatest coach and number one cheerleader. She is in your corner holding up the pom poms. Seriously.

I see what culture is throwing at you. Even though I am no longer in your shoes, I am *constantly* listening to your voice. I make it my goal not just to speak to young people, but to also listen so I am able to *better* relate and connect. This is no time for adults to disconnect from your generation. We need to be able to talk the same language so that we can really see eye to eye and help you navigate the countless decisions that are being thrown at you every single day. The fact that you are reading this and are gearing up to do this study with your mom means that your mom *desires* to speak your language. She sincerely wants to help you to become the woman God has designed and destined you to be. This is not a study about restriction or limitations. It's about value. It's about *you* knowing how precious you are to your Father in Heaven, to your family on earth, and ultimately it's about meeting a Boaz who will also recognize that value.

This *study* is designed to help you connect with your mother in a way that few daughters do, and, I pray, be a stepping-stone toward a much more honest, open, and authentic relationship between the two of you. Believe me, you are going to need it when Bozo comes a-knocking. Whether you have a great relationship already where there are no secrets or you feel closed off from one another, like you two are living on different planets—my prayer is that by going through this book and workbook together, something special takes place in your relationship.

Okay, so I am not one to be vague. The something special I want to see happen is that *your mom* becomes your teacher, cheerleader, coach, and spiritual monitor. Your friends might not be bragging on their parents and the influence they have in their lives, but according to an extensive study conducted by *USA Today Weekend Magazine*, 70 percent of 272,400 polled teenagers identified their parents as the most important influence in their lives. Wow! Not media. Not peers. Not school. Not church. Yeah, your mom!

If these statistics are true, you have an awesome and exciting opportunity standing before you.

Here is what I would like you to do next: Read the preface to *Raising a Lady in Waiting*. It gives you a glimpse of my personal story, and also shares the reason why I believe this message is so important for moms to share with their daughters. Then you will begin your interactive journey alongside your mom. You will read the book, and she will read the book. You will fill out your workbook, and then she will fill out her workbook. You will do the readings and exercises separately, only because I expect both of you are tremendously busy.

That said, we can't make busyness our "go to" excuse for everything. It can become a god if we are not careful. At the end of each week, you and your mother will come together for a time of sharing, mentorship, and authentic relationship building. You will have the opportunity to talk, openly and honestly, about the topic you both studied that week and share anything from your workbook experience that might help you along the journey to becoming a *lady in waiting*.

Above all, my prayer is that you, young lady in waiting, would be a pursuer of the Lord Jesus Christ *above all else*. As He is the most important relationship in your life, I can assure you, everything else will come into its place. You will need coaching along the way, absolutely. We all do through this journey. That said, when you are first and foremost one sold out to King Jesus, it will become *very difficult* for you to give your heart away to anyone, *anyone* who treats you in a way that your King would disapprove of.

Here's to the journey ahead. I am so thrilled. So excited. So expectant that a great God is going to do great things in both of your lives!

Much love,

Jackie

How to Use This Workbook

Here are some tips on how to use this workbook for yourself, work with your mother through the chapters of the book/workbook sessions, and get the most out of this experience that you possibly can.

A Note on the Time Commitment

When it comes to the time commitment required, I stress *quality over quantity*. I know you are both busy people. You are busy going to school, having a social life, doing sports—all normal and totally cool.

I'm also confident that your mother has a pretty busy social calendar, where raising a family, working, having her own social life, and other things like that may be taking up a good portion of her time.

The exercises in this workbook should not take you more than 15 to 20 minutes per day. Again, it is so important that in the middle of our busyness we do not neglect the most important things. The investment that your mom wants to make in your life is one of the most precious and important things you could ever imagine. Consider that when it comes to doing this study.

Breakdown

Weekly Video Coaching Tip from Jackie

If possible, watch this together—mom and daughter. If not, both of you can watch it separately, but it would be best for you to listen the clip together. For about ten minutes, I am going to *coach* you on what to expect in that week's session, and what you should expect to get out of it—mom *and* daughter. I will leave you with an *encouragement.* It might be in the form of a testimony. Maybe it will be a life lesson I have learned along the journey, or a testimony someone shared with me. After watching this, you will be ready to take on the week!

Daily Readings from Raising a Lady in Waiting

Read your daily segment(s) from *Raising a Lady in Waiting* as provided in each session. This will help you go through the book at a comfortable pace and digest all the major ideas that are presented. Every day, you will be assigned to read a certain section of the chapter and answer daily reflection questions.

Each chapter will be broken into five daily sections. It is recommended that you do the readings/daily discussion questions on Monday through Friday, so that you can devote one of the weekend days to spend time with your mother and review the material you covered. While this specific schedule is not essential, we find that this particular method tends to work best to promote the overall goal of the exercises.

Daily Reflection Questions

Each section will have corresponding Daily Reflection Questions designed to get you interacting with the material. These questions will actually coincide with what your mother is reading and responding to in her workbook.

The goal is that you will: 1) read the book, 2) go through the workbook activities, and 3) at the end of the week, be able to have an honest, open, real discussion about what you have been going through in the workbook.

Daily Prayer for Daughter/Mother

Principles without prayer are just informational tidbits. Prayer adds substance and power to what we are doing here. I want you to be praying for God's direction in shaping your life as you take this journey to become a young lady in waiting.

Also, keep in mind these prayers are designed to help, not hinder, your personal prayer life. In other words, we want to give you some type of example prayer to pray—not to be the be all and end all of your prayer life, but as something to jump-start your prayer focus for the day. We must be focused in our prayers, especially when it comes to seeing God doing specific things in our lives.

Mother-Daughter Time

At the end of the week, preferably on Saturday or Sunday, mom and daughter will spend some time together. Maybe grab lunch somewhere or coffee at Starbucks. This exercise is not designed to be some cold, distant, "What do *you* learn about?" Okay. Got it. Now, "What did *you* learn about going through this book?" Okay. Cool. Are we done now? Time to go off to separate ends of life again.

Perhaps other devotionals and books have made this kind of forced kind of conversation easy in the past, but quite honestly, I didn't have the time to put together this material so that moms and daughters just made it another "must do" on the list. You are going through this material because you recognize the *value* and the *investment.*

I am going to present this material in a very simple way for you to use it however you feel comfortable. Basically, I am giving you a set of questions for both you and your mother to answer—*together.* If either of you don't feel like you can answer a certain question, don't worry! Answer it based on what you *think* should be the right answer after going through that section in *Raising a Lady in Waiting.* Use this time to talk. Talk about what you read. Talk about some of the exercises you went through. Were they a struggle? Were there certain questions that you could not answer? Were there questions that you could answer and *were excited* about the answer? I don't want to give *too much* structure here, as this needs to be real. Again, I'll simply give you a list of questions to help guide your discussion. The rest is up to you!

Week 1

INTRODUCTION SESSION

Lady in Waiting is not about finding the right man,
but becoming the right woman.

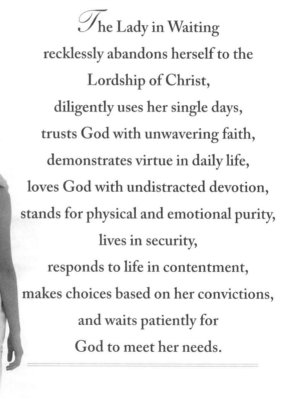

The Lady in Waiting
recklessly abandons herself to the
Lordship of Christ,
diligently uses her single days,
trusts God with unwavering faith,
demonstrates virtue in daily life,
loves God with undistracted devotion,
stands for physical and emotional purity,
lives in security,
responds to life in contentment,
makes choices based on her convictions,
and waits patiently for
God to meet her needs.

Day One

INTRODUCTION

Read: *RALIW* Introduction, pages 21-23 (Read up until the *Ideal Mom, Former Prostitute* heading.)

The principles in this book are intended to guard and to guide: To guard you from a Bozo guy and to guide you toward a man worth waiting for—a modern Boaz.

DAILY REFLECTION QUESTIONS

1. In general, why do you believe it is so important to guard your heart from a "Bozo" guy?

2. When you read the phrase, "Bozo" guy, what does that mean to you?

3. How does the man whom you end up with—either a Bozo or a Boaz—actually determine the course of your future?

____

____

____

____

DAILY PRAYER

Father, guide me toward Your perfect plan for my life. Help me to take what I am learning in this book and apply it to my everyday life.

Holy Spirit, open my heart to hear Your voice and stir me to pursue Your perfect plan for my life.

In Jesus' Name, Amen.

Day Two

IDEAL MOM—FORMER PROSTITUTE

Read: *RALIW* Introduction, page 23 (Read the *Ideal Mom—Former Prostitute* section.)

If by any chance you think it is too late—be encouraged. The breath in your nostrils is proof of the hope that God is not finished with you yet.

DAILY REFLECTION QUESTIONS

1. Go on to read about Rahab in Joshua 2. This former prostitute would become the mother of Boaz, the leading man in the love story of Ruth. What message does Rahab's story speak to someone who believes she has messed up beyond fixing or has made one too many poor choices in her life?

2. How does this specifically speak to you?

Daily Prayer

Lord, thank You for Your grace. You are the God of second chances, and third chances, and one thousandth chances. Nothing exhausts Your grace, Your mercy, and Your kindness.

I know I have made mistakes in the past. I may be making them right now. Instead of giving up, I push forward. I reject the enemy's lie that it is "too late." The fact that I am alive and breathing means there is hope that You are not finished with me and that you have amazing plans for my life.

In Jesus' Name, Amen.

Day Three

VITAL COLLEGE PREP COURSE

Read: *RALIW* Introduction, pages 23-24 (Read the *Vital College Prep Course* section.)

I know too many kids who are passing school and flunking life in their relationships.

DAILY REFLECTION QUESTIONS

1. Why do you think young people (yes, even those who go to Christian schools and are attending church) are making unwise and horrible choices in their everyday lives?

2. What does this statement mean to you: "Too many kids are passing school and flunking life in their relationships"?

3. Why it is important that you learn to actually *live out* what is written in this book, rather than just reading it?

____

____

____

____

Daily Prayer

God, I ask You to protect me from the poor choices available to me daily.

I don't want to just read a book; I want to see my life changed. I want to be the young woman Jackie writes about. Help me to make good choices based on what I am reading about and what is written in Your Word.

Show me, Lord, that right choices are for my good. I know they are not always popular and are definitely not easy to make. However, remind me that making right choices shows the world that I value myself.

In Jesus' Name, Amen.

Day Four

"CLIFF NOTES"

Read: *RALIW* Introduction, pages 24-25
(Read the *Cliff Notes for Mom* section.)

You can consider this the "Cliff Notes" from my decades of searching for transferrable concepts to help mothers raise girls who will not become Bozo magnets.

DAILY REFLECTION QUESTIONS

1. Just as I have written this book out of my past experience, learning a thing or two about judging the difference between a Boaz and a Bozo, I think it is very important for you to stop and consider your personal "cliff notes." Think of times in your life when you were pursued by a Bozo. Did you end up giving in to the pursuit? Why or why not?

2. Where are you right now (in your relationship journey)? Are you "crushing" on a boy at school? Are you currently in a relationship? Has your heart already been broken by a Bozo?

DAILY PRAYER

Lord, I ask for Your help wherever I am along the journey. Thank You for strength to not only deal with what I am struggling with, but also, for opening up my relationship with mom so that we can walk through this journey together.

In Jesus' Name, Amen.

Day Five

GUIDEBOOK FOR PARIS... AND PARENTING

Read: *RALIW* Introduction, pages 25-29 (Read the *Guidebook for Paris and Parenting* section, take your *Prep Quiz,* and read the information that follows.)

I feel like this book will be a helpful tour guidebook as you maneuver through the challenges of becoming a Young Lady in Waiting and avoiding the tyranny of a becoming a Bozo magnet.

DAILY REFLECTION QUESTIONS

1. Why is it important to keep your standards high?

Before moving on, I recommend doing the *Daily Prayer* and then turning over to the *Prep Quiz for Moms.* This is available at the end of the Introduction chapter in the book. Even though this Prep Quiz is designed for moms, it would be a good idea for you to go through the questions as well and honestly answer them.

DAILY PRAYER

Lord, prepare my heart to answer the following questions honestly. Whether I score well or poorly, I refuse to get discouraged and feel like a failure. Give me a teachable heart so that I can change in the ways You want me to.

Above all, help me to keep my eyes fixed on Jesus, the Unchanging One. I am so thankful He remains my Rock of safety no matter what life brings.

In the weeks to come, help me increase my trust and confidence in Jesus, that He would be my source of strength.

In Jesus' Name, Amen.

Together

MOTHER/DAUGHTER SESSION

INSTRUCTIONS

You have both gone through the introduction in both the book and workbook. Here are some of the questions you can discuss during your first mother-daughter session:

- What does Jackie mean when she talks about a "Bozo" guy versus a Boaz?
- What does the story of Rahab the prostitute say to you about the people God uses to do great things?
- Why is it so important to keep high standards?
- What are some of the things that culture, society, and other people say about women who have high standards?
- Deep down, do you think that women with high standards are ultimately looked down on or admired (even if they are secretly admired)?
- What are some of the benefits of keeping your standards high and not giving in to compromise?
- What did you think of the prep quiz?
- Were there certain questions that didn't make sense? If so, which ones? (Most likely, these are the questions that used phrases we will be talking about in the weeks ahead.)

Week 2

Becoming a Young Lady of Reckless Abandon

As daughters of the King who gave Himself for us, we are to give ourselves to Him, leaving the world, giving up our strategies, and withdrawing support from the wiles of the devil and the ways of the flesh. Reckless abandon is how we fling ourselves toward God and utterly forsake our sinful nature.

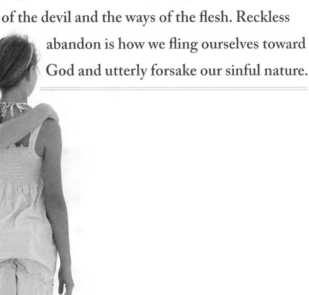

Day One

THE "SHOUT YES" LIFESTYLE

Read: *RALIW* Chapter 1, pages 31-33 (Read *Ruth's Reckless Abandon* and *The Shout Yes Mom* sections.)

Saying "Yes" to God is an act of daily surrender and a display of one's own reckless abandon.

DAILY REFLECTION QUESTIONS

1. What does reckless abandon look like to God? Consider the example of Ruth and Naomi. How did Ruth demonstrate reckless abandon to God, and how can you follow her example in your life?

2. How do you model a "Shout Yes" lifestyle to God?

3. What are some specific ways your life can say "Yes" to God?

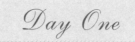

DAILY PRAYER

May my life shout yes to You, Jesus. Every decision, every thought, every attitude and action—I pray that they would say "Yes" to Your will, Your plan, and Your purpose.

Lord, may my reckless abandon to You speak to my generation. May it model a lifestyle that others are hungry to walk in and experience for themselves. I thank You that doing what You say releases Your blessing and Your purpose into my life. There is nothing else that satisfies like walking in Your perfect will for my life. Thank You for the ability to do this, even in a world that tries so hard to distract me and keep me from doing what You want.

In Jesus' Name, Amen.

Day Two

GOD'S VESSELS

Read: *RALIW* Chapter 1, pages 34-37 (Read *Dateless Friday Night Miracles* and *Maddie and Libby's Story* sections.)

Reckless abandon is a level of surrender that unlocks the greatest treasures God has in store for His kids.

DAILY REFLECTION QUESTIONS

1. Based on what Jackie experienced during her *Dateless Friday Night Miracle*, what are some benefits to saying "No" to certain things and "Yes" to God?

2. Do you feel like you are growing spiritually? What are some noticeable signs of your spiritual growth? What would your friends and family say if they were asked about your spiritual growth?

3. What is Mom doing to *passionately* encourage your relationship with the Lord? If she isn't doing anything, or seems to be doing the wrong things—what would you say to her?

____

____

____

____

DAILY PRAYER

Lord, help me to keep the first things first in prayer. Help me to make my most important focus be a passionate relationship with You. Show me how I can go after You, God, above everything else. Not using a bunch of rules, regulations, and laws. Show me how to be hungry for You, Jesus.

In His Name, Amen.

Day Three

PREGNANT WITH MESSIAH

Read: *RALIW* Chapter 1, page 38 (Read *Your Daughter Pregnant with Messiah!* section.)

The safest place to be is the place where you are more concerned about what God thinks than what anybody else thinks.

DAILY REFLECTION QUESTIONS

1. How have you observed your mother saying "Yes" to God with reckless abandon? List examples of times when your mother has obediently followed the Lord in spite of what anyone else thought.

2. How does the example of Mary, the mother of Jesus, give us a model for the lifestyle of reckless abandon that God wants us to walk in?

Daily Prayer

Father, I know you have incredible plans and dreams for me. You have things planned for me that can only be accomplished by Your mighty hand working in and through my life. I pray right now that You would strengthen me with the obedience and reckless abandon of Mary. You found her fit to give birth to Jesus, and Lord, I pray that You would entrust me with giving "birth" to Your plans and purposes on Earth. Help me silence voices of opposition and compromise that try to distract me from Your plans.

In Jesus' Name, Amen.

Day Four

THE SECRET OF THE ALABASTER BOX

Read: *RALIW* Chapter 1, pages 38-41 (Read *Secret of the Alabaster Box* section.)

This sinner had her dreams, and she wisely broke her alabaster box in the presence of the only One who can make a woman's dreams come true.

DAILY REFLECTION QUESTIONS

1. Read Luke 7:36-50. When you read about this sinful woman who broke such a valuable possession over the feet of Jesus, what does this act say to you about being a young woman of reckless abandon?

2. Have you already broken your alabaster box at the feet of someone not worthy of what's inside? Or is it sealed shut, awaiting the man worthy of the box's precious contents?

Note: This is not necessarily in regard to sexual purity, but rather opening up your life, your hopes, and your dreams to someone who did not regard those things as precious and valuable, and ultimately treated them as worthless.

3. How can you give your dreams to God, entrusting them to Him *alone*?

DAILY PRAYER

Father, I ask that You show me how precious my dreams are—that they are not worthy of being poured out before anyone, especially someone who does not value them. Protect me, Lord. Protect me from those who would treat all of the treasures You have put in my life as worthless. I ask that You protect me by showing me my value to You.

In Jesus' Name, Amen.

Day Five

DAUGHTERS WHO LISTEN TO THEIR HEAVENLY PAPA

Read: *RALIW* Chapter 1, pages 42-43 (Read *Raising Daughters Who Listen to Their Heavenly Papa* section.)

Your trained capacity to hear and obey God will profoundly impact your journey on planet earth and help you to discover God's best for you life.

DAILY REFLECTION QUESTIONS

1. In view of the story about Gerta and her boots, why is instant and complete obedience to God so important?

____

____

____

____

2. On a scale of 1 to 10, how would you rate your level of swift obedience to God?

1	2	3	4	5	6	7	8	9	10

3. How do you model *swift obedience* to your heavenly Papa?

DAILY PRAYER

You are Lord and Master. May my life be an example of someone who obeys You quickly and completely.
Even when I fail and miss it, Holy Spirit, use that as a teachable moment that pushes me toward a lifestyle of instant obedience to a trustworthy Father.

In Jesus' Name, Amen.

Basic Instructions from Papa

1. Love the Lord your God with all your heart, soul, and mind (see Matt. 22:37).
2. Love your neighbor as yourself (see Matt. 22:39).
3. Make the Kingdom of God your primary concern (see Matt. 6:33).
4. Be anxious for nothing (see Phil. 4:6).
5. Pray without ceasing (see 1 Thess. 5:17).
6. Be a student of the Word (see 2 Tim. 2:15).
7. In everything give thanks (see 1 Thess. 5:18).
8. Forgive as freely as you have been forgiven by Christ (see Eph. 4:32).
9. Esteem others more important than yourself (see Phil. 2:3-4).
10. Say "Yes" to God's script rather than clinging to your own agenda (see Luke 1:37-38).

Together

MOTHER/DAUGHTER SESSION

INSTRUCTIONS

You have both gone through Week 2 in the workbook (which covered Chapter 1 in the book). The focus of this week was your relationship with God. Here are some of the questions you can discuss during your mother-daughter session.

Ask *each other* these honest questions:

- Why is it so important to immediately obey God's voice?
- Has God ever told you to do something, and you hesitated? What happened?
- What does reckless abandon to God look like?
- Who are some people you know who would fit the description "recklessly abandoned to God" (both alive today and back in the Bible times)?
- What are some of the benefits of being abandoned to God?
- Mom and Daughter—share testimonies of times you both have obeyed God instantly and watched Him do incredible things in your lives.
- What are some ways that you both can grow in your personal relationship with God?

This exercise is not about making anyone feel unspiritual or bad about their relationship with God. The wonderful thing is the Father is calling all of us deeper. All of us need to step up our level of reckless abandon, and as we do we will see God "step up" the blessing in our lives.

Week 3

Becoming a Young Lady of Diligence

A holy hug, some encouraging words, an open heart and home, a willingness to serve, and a heart bent toward our Lord in prayer—these are worthy exercises to practice and to build into our lives. These are the actions and the fruits that make you a Young Lady of Diligence.

Day One

HUMILITY AND DILIGENCE: QUALIFICATIONS OF A WORLD-CHANGER

Read: *RALIW* Chapter 2, pages 45-47 (Read *Ruth's Diligence* and *Humility and Diligence: Qualifications of a World-Changer* sections.)

Diligence fortifies a person with the capacity to continue long after everyone else has quit, either because the task was too hard or not satisfying enough.

DAILY REFLECTION QUESTIONS

1. How does the story of Ruth and her work ethic model diligence to you?

____

____

____

____

2. Why is diligence such an important attribute to develop as a young lady in waiting?

____

____

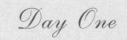

3. List some areas in your life that are examples of diligence. Celebrate them! Likewise, what are some areas you need to develop further?

Daily Prayer

Lord, thank You for what I can achieve by practicing diligence. Accomplishment. Character. Endurance. Perseverance. Thank You for teaching me how to have diligence in my life.

Show me the areas in my life that have not been given to diligence. Holy Spirit, empower me to confront these areas and, by Your grace, make the necessary changes.

In Jesus' Name, Amen.

Day Two

DILIGENCE AND INTERNAL JOGGING

Read: *RALIW* Chapter 2, pages 47-48 (Read *Diligence and Internal Jogging* section.) The remainder of this week, we are going to focus on some essential characteristics of a Young Lady of Diligence. On some days, we will go through two to three topics. Today, we are starting with and focusing on one of most essential—prayer.

The prayer life of a Young Lady of Diligence can be life-impacting from a very young age. As with physical exercise, the only way to fail at prayer is to fail to show up.

DAILY REFLECTION QUESTIONS

1. How does the phrase "internal jogging" relate to your prayer life?

2. How can you develop a prayer life where everything is "on the table" and you are encouraged to pray about anything?

3. Do you currently experience this type of openness and freedom with God in your prayer life? If not, *why not?*

4. Based on First Thessalonians 5:17, what does it mean to "pray continually"? How can you practice a lifestyle of continuous prayer?

DAILY PRAYER

Father, I pray for a free and open prayer life, where You and I talk about everything and anything. Nothing is off limits and everything is something we can talk about. Show me how to do this kind of prayer with You. Change the way I think about prayer. If I see it as boring, dull, and just another spiritual chore, help me to see it as something that is full of life, power, and passion.

In Jesus Name, Amen.

Day Three

A HOLY HIT LIST AND PRAYING FOR YOUR CRUSHES

Read: *RALIW* Chapter 2, page 49 (Read *A Holy Hit List* and *Diligent Prayer for Your "Crushes"* sections.)

Praying for those who need Jesus is a most holy habit.

DAILY REFLECTION QUESTIONS

1. What does it mean to make a "holy hit list"? Have you ever done something like this before? (Maybe using a different name for it?) If so, what results did you see?

When you are "crushing" on a certain boy, then pray for him. Such prayers are a wonderful "heart guard"!

2. List some benefits of diligently praying for the boys you are "crushing on."

3. How can praying for these boys position God to speak to you about your "crushes"? What might He tell you?

DAILY PRAYER

Thank You, Lord, that prayer is not just for me to wish that something good might happen—prayer is the greatest thing I can do to make things happen! Show me the importance of making a list of those who need Jesus. Help me to diligently pray for their salvations—and celebrate when they come to know You! Give me names to put on this list and words to pray over their lives as the Holy Spirit is working.

And Lord, when there is a boy I like—help me have the confidence to tell my mother about the way that I feel. Help us, together, to diligently pray for his needs, family, and any specific situations going on in his life, as well as seek Your will in this relationship.

In Jesus' Name, Amen.

Day Four

HOLY SWEAT AND PIGGY BANKS

Read: *RALIW* Chapter 2, pages 50-52 (Read *Diligence and Holy Sweat* and *Diligence and Breaking One's Piggy Bank* sections.)

Working up a holy sweat of service is an offering to God—a "sweat offering" that will come back as a blessing upon your heart.

DAILY REFLECTION QUESTIONS

1. How do you work up a "holy sweat" in your life? (Examples: household chores, church services, community involvement, etc.)

2. How can you re-shape your view of service by showing it to be a blessing and not a curse? (Read Proverbs 31:10-31 for some pointers.)

> Nothing is more touching than to see a young person give of her limited funds to a needy cause—whether in church, school, or community.

3. How can you practice being unselfish in giving to the needs of others, particularly those who are less fortunate?

___

___

___

4. How can you be unselfish with your family and friends? (See Proverbs 31:20.)

___

___

___

___

DAILY PRAYER

Father, show me how to live a life of service and selflessness.

Holy Spirit, help me see places in my life that do not have diligent service and selflessness and I need to change.

In Jesus' Name, Amen.

Day Five

HALLMARK CARDS, JUNK-FOOD DRAWERS, AND HOLY HUGS

Read: *RALIW* Chapter 2, pages 52-57 (Read *Diligence and Hallmark Cards*, *Diligence and a Junk-Food Drawer*, and *Diligence and Holy Hugs* sections.)

Whether e-mailing, texting, or even writing a card, God's girls can keep hope alive in the hearts of those they love—simply by being cheerleaders of truth!

DAILY REFLECTION QUESTIONS

1. How do you try to be an encouragement to others? Is this something that comes naturally to you, or do you need some guidance?

2. How would you currently rate your mother's hospitality? How can your mom create a culture of hospitality in your home that impacts you and your friends?

A good hug is a gift to the human heart. It doesn't require special training, a college degree, or a bank account. Yet the benefits are priceless.

3. Are you prone to hug people, or are you a more hands-off type of person? How would the simple act of hugging people show love and kindness?

Daily Prayer

Lord, I invite You to fill my heart with kindness, genuine love, and concern toward people. Let this love be so clear and overwhelming that I will want to show Your love toward those who need it in real, physical ways—saying encouraging things, hospitality, or loving hugs.

In Jesus' Name, Amen.

Together

MOTHER/DAUGHTER SESSION

INSTRUCTIONS

You have both gone through Week 3 in the workbook (which covered Chapter 2 in the book). The focus of this week was diligence. Here are some of the questions you can discuss during your mother-daughter session.

1. What does "diligence" mean to the *both of you*?

2. How does being diligent impact the following areas of life?

   - Prayer life
   - Relationships
   - Work
   - Serving other people

3. Are there areas in your lives where you can say, "Yes, I am diligent," or "No, I need some help on being diligent with that"?

4. What do you think are the benefits of being diligent are?

5. For example, what happens when you are diligent in the following situations?

   - Diligent to pray for the guys you like (daughter).
   - Diligent to encourage your friends and family members.
   - Diligent to serve others (in church, community, etc.)
   - Diligent to use your money to help other people.

6. Based on First Thessalonians 5:17, what does it look like to be diligent in prayer?

One of the greatest ways we can practice diligence is through prayer. Paul tells us to pray *continually* or *without ceasing* (see 1 Thess. 5:17). Take this time to pray about specific needs or people whom you want to commit to diligently pray for. Write their names down somewhere visible where you can constantly be reminded to pray for them.

As you watch God move in these situations and people, it is so important to track the progress, write it down, and then celebrate it together. Focusing on testimonies of God's faithfulness in answering prayer (that you participated in!) actually strengthens our diligence.

Week 4

Becoming a Young Lady of Faith

You can make a difference in this world through the daily growing of your faith in our incomparable God. Just because you may be too young to date doesn't mean it's too early to train your heart toward the Lover of your Soul.

Day One

GETTING YOUR SEVEN

Read: *RALIW* Chapter 3, pages 59-63 (Read *Ruth's Faith, Getting Her "Seven" Daily*, and *Do I Need to Repeat Myself? Yes!* Sections.)

I took the instruction to "get my seven" very seriously, and actually couldn't wait to read my Bible. From that day until this day, I have never "recovered" from this privilege.

DAILY REFLECTION QUESTIONS

1. Why is it so important for you to spend daily time in the Scriptures?

2. How does reading God's Word—*even if it's just for seven minutes a day*—build and strengthen your faith? (See Romans 10:17.)

3. In what ways do you "repeat" the Word of God, communicating its truths to others on a regular basis? Why do you think it is so important to constantly be hearing God's Word in a variety of ways? (See Deuteronomy 6:5-7.)

DAILY PRAYER

Lord, I want to love Your Word even more than I do now. Show me ways to constantly keep the true meaning of Scripture in front of my eyes. Help me grow in faith as I commit to spending time in the Scriptures daily—even if it's only for seven minutes.
Thank You for the power and promises contained in its pages.

In Jesus' Name, Amen.

Day Two

NO-BOZO HEART GUARD

Read: *RALIW* Chapter 3, pages 63-64 (Read *A No-Bozo Heart Guard* section.)

Your consistency is invaluable. The challenges you are facing in life require strong faith, and faith is inextricably linked to one's daily "face time" with God.

DAILY REFLECTION QUESTIONS

1. What practical results has studying God's Word produced in your life?

2. How can constantly feeding your heart on the Word of God set you up to *avoid* making bad relationship decisions?

3. What are some ways you pursue God's Word—even if it's just for seven minutes a day?

____

____

____

____

Daily Prayer

Lord, I pray that You would teach me to love reading the Bible because it is Your Word. Also, help my relationship with You be unmistakable to other people. If there are things that need changing in my life, show them to me and help me change. I know You don't show me where I need to change because I am a bad person. You're not angry or upset with me. You are simply helping me to become a better, happier person, something I have not experienced before. Thank You, Lord, for all You give me in Your Word. Open my eyes to the life-changing truths contained in its pages, and encourage me to go after everything You want to share with me.

In Jesus' Name, Amen.

Day Three

OVERCOMING THE DISTRACTION OF BUSYNESS

Read: *RALIW* Chapter 3, pages 65-67 (Read *Too Busy to "Get Your Seven"* section.)

If you think you are too busy to read the Bible, I promise you, you aren't.

DAILY REFLECTION QUESTIONS

1. Why do you feel too busy to read the Bible? Even if you have incorporated regular Bible reading time into your lifestyle, have you ever felt this way? If so, why?

2. How could you benefit from "quiet time" with God in the Scriptures? Think of some specific examples of times you have enjoyed time with the Lord in His Word. What made these times so enjoyable? (These are the benefits you should share with your mother during your weekly time together!)

3. Do you have a regular quiet time with God? If not, what are some ways you can incorporate quiet time into your life?

Daily Prayer

Father, I ask for guidance to see the benefits and blessings of spending time with You—in Your Presence and in Your Word. I want our time together to be really special, something that only You and I share and that I look forward to every day. Also, show me some simple ways to help me spend time with You and enjoy the benefits of a deep relationship with You.

In Jesus' Name, Amen.

Day Four

YOU CAN'T SMUDGE HIM OUT

Read: *RALIW* Chapter 3, pages 67-71 (Read *Ruth and a Kidnapped Girl—Two Hearts of Faith* and *You Can't Smudge Him Out* sections.)

I have told so many people that God can use them even during their darkest hours when their faith has been outrun by their pain and bitterness has crept into their hearts!

DAILY REFLECTION QUESTIONS

1. Read Ruth 1:16. How did Ruth's faith motivate her to leave behind her old life (and old gods) and follow the God of Israel? How would this faith ultimately lead her to meeting Boaz?

2. Read Second Kings 5:1-4. How did faith in God protect the young Israelite girl (who was kidnapped) from letting bitterness and unforgiveness define her?

3. How can God still use you, even in your darkest hours? Can you recall times when, in spite of bitterness, anger, unforgiveness, or pain, God still used you to minister to someone?

DAILY PRAYER

God, thank You for using broken people. Thank You for using me! For all of those times when I messed up or when I was sad, mad, frustrated, unforgiving, bitter—all of that—thank You that Your light continues to shine through the darkness, revealing You to someone in need.

In Jesus' Name, Amen.

Day Five

STUDYING THE WORD, GROWING YOUR FAITH

Read: *RALIW* Chapter 3, pages 71-74 (Read *Q.T. Kiss Method for You and Your Daughter, Jesus Calling, Red Circle of Trust, One Year Bible Method,* and *Incomparable Benefit of Bible Reading: Growing Faith* sections.)

Just because you are too young to date doesn't mean it's too early to train your heart toward the Lover of your Soul.

DAILY REFLECTION QUESTIONS

1. Which of the Bible study options presented sound most appealing to you? If you are already on a Bible study program, which one are you currently using and what benefits have you been experiencing as a result?

2. How will developing habits of spending time in the Word actually strengthen your faith? How will this impact the decisions you make and keep you strong through difficulty?

3. Specifically, how will your growing and maturing faith protect you as you enter the relationship world?

Daily Prayer

Father, thanks for growing and maturing my faith when I spend time reading the Bible. Again, show me how to pursue Your Word in a deeper way. Help me to avoid letting it feel superficial or like some type of obligation. In fact, show me how to clearly share the benefits and joy and peace and power and wisdom that come from being connected to Your Word.

Take me, Lord, and develop me into a woman of strong faith—faith that keeps me strong through every situation of life, keeping me safe in Your truth, Your love, and Your unending faithfulness.

In Jesus' Name, Amen.

KEYS TO EFFECTIVE BIBLE STUDY

Practical preparation for your quiet time:

- The same chair
- The same Bible
- The same journal (journal in composition book, journal book, or the Bible margins)
- A notepad
- The same pen
- Study helps nearby—ESV Study Bible for the hard questions

What Is Available Daily in God's Word?

(From Psalm 119)

- Wonderful truths (see verse 18)
- Wise advice (see verse 24)
- Encouragement for the discouraged (see verse 25)
- Hope for those in grief and despair (see verse 28)
- Discernment between worthy and worthless things (see verse 37)
- Wisdom beyond one's years (see verses 99-100)
- Insight to spot false belief systems (see verses 104, 130)
- Rest and peace for the weary soul (see verse 165)

Together

MOTHER/DAUGHTER SESSION

INSTRUCTIONS

You have both gone through Week 4 in the workbook (which covered Chapter 3 in the book). The focus of this week was faith. Here are some of the questions you can discuss during your mother-daughter session:

- What are the benefits to spending time in God's Word?
- When the phrase "spending time with God" is used, what comes to your mind? Is it boring and dull? Is it sitting in a room, reading a book?
- If you have a negative impression of what "spending time with God" looks like, in what ways can you start changing the way you interact with God?
- How does spending time in God's Word build up your faith?
- How does spending time in God's Word cause you to avoid making bad decisions?
- In what ways have you both experienced God's Word actually protecting you from making a bad choice?
- Do you feel like you have time to read the Bible? Are you both too busy? If so, how could you arrange your schedules to spend more time in God's Word?

- What are some ways that would help you read the Bible more often? What do you think about the "Seven Daily" program? Is this a method that would help both of you stay in the Word more consistently?

I would like both of you to commit to this: Take the next seven weeks (for the remainder of this study) and spend at least *seven minutes* in God's Word each day. Don't try to push for more or settle for less.

I know you're busy. God knows you're busy! That said, I really pray that, after reading this chapter on raising (and becoming) a young lady of faith, you see the benefit of spending time with God—in His Word and Presence.

Week 5

BECOMING A YOUNG LADY OF VIRTUE

The leading man in the Book of Ruth was drawn to the leading lady because of the obvious virtue displayed in her life through her choices. In modern times like these, virtue is not what most guys are concerned about; they are often too busy looking at the exterior and are not even concerned about the interior.

Day One

WHAT DOES VIRTUE LOOK LIKE?

Read: *RALIW* Chapter 4, pages 77-81 (Read *Ruth's Virtue, Is Virtue Extinct in the 21st Century,* and *You Are More Than Your Breast Size.*)

A woman of virtue is irresistible to a godly man. Virtue is a pearl worth pursuing.

DAILY REFLECTION QUESTIONS

1. What is your understanding of virtue? How does Ruth model this virtue in Ruth 2:10-11, thus making herself attractive to Boaz?

2. How can you develop virtuous qualities that do *not* attract the wrong type of guy?

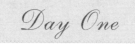

3. How much do you pay attention to what you wear and how you present yourself? How does what you wear communicate a message to guys (who are looking)?

____

____

____

____

DAILY PRAYER

Father, thank You for the blessing and reward of knowing the difference between right and wrong. Give me eyes to see what I am wearing, how other people see me even when I may not know it, and what kind of girl they think I am.
Help me to confidently see my value so that I feel no need to wear things in the wrong ways in front of the wrong people.
Above all, help me to see the value that You have placed on me—Your daughter.

In Jesus' Name, Amen.

Day Two

WHY MODESTY?

Read: *RALIW* Chapter 4, pages 81-83 (Read *Help with Modesty for Moms* and *Modesty and Little Girls* sections.)

Do you have a consecrated closet? Do you dress modestly, or are you eye candy for the boys as well as the men around you?

DAILY REFLECTION QUESTIONS

1. What does the following quote say to you about modesty: *"Modesty is presenting yourself so that the attention of other people is drawn to your face"*?

2. How can/do you show that you live modestly?

3. Read First Corinthians 6:19-20. How does recognizing that we are temples of the Holy Spirit change the way we think about modesty?

DAILY PRAYER

Father, I pray You would continue to show me that as a Christian I am a temple of the Holy Spirit. Your holy Presence lives inside of me. I have been saved to not only go to Heaven one day, but to represent Jesus here on earth today.

Show me how I am special and what I offer the world as Your daughter filled with the Presence of King Jesus. The more I realize who You are, the more I will present myself modestly.

In Jesus' Name, Amen.

Day Three

WHO I DATE REFLECTS WHO I AM

Read: *RALIW* Chapter 4, pages 83-86 (Read *Who Do Young Ladies of Virtue Date?* and *Toothpicks in Eyeballs* sections.)

Dating is not simply a social activity. Who you want to date is a reflection of your depth, spiritually speaking. You need to pay attention to which boys you are crushing on, because it reveals your heart.

DAILY REFLECTION QUESTIONS

1. Based on Second Corinthians 6:14, why is it important that Christians date other believers? (Even if it is only just "one date.")

2. How can dating a believer (who is *actually* passionate for the Lord Jesus Christ and not just "Christian" in title only) set you up for the future?

3. How do the guys you want to date reflect your spiritual depth? Why is it important that you pay attention to the kinds of guys you want to date?

Daily Prayer

Lord, help me be aware of the types of guys I want to date. Show me what this means about where I am in my relationship with You.
If I am going after the wrong guys, Lord, help me to see my value and not settle by dating someone who does not know You or who is not serious about You.
Above all, I pray that my relationship with You is the most important thing in my life.
In His Name, Amen.

Day Four

THE GREAT SELF-DECEPTION

Read: *RALIW* Chapter 4, pages 86-88 (Read *Greatest Self-Deception—Missionary Dating* and *Even Ninth-Grade Boys Know This* sections.)

A common self-deception among girls as well as women is the power that the girl thinks she has to change the one she has a crush on, admires from afar, or has begun to date.

DAILY REFLECTION QUESTIONS

1. How is it deceiving for you to think that you can change the guys you have a crush on—believing that you can lead these guys into a relationship with Jesus simply by dating them?

____

____

____

____

2. In what ways is a believer who dates a non-believer blatantly disobeying the clear commands of the Lord? (See 2 Corinthians 6:14.)

____

____

3. Why is it self-deception to think you can change another person's behavior?

Daily Prayer

Lord, protect me from believing the lie that I can change a guy. Only You change hearts, Holy Spirit.

Show me that the best thing I could possibly do is wait for someone who believes the same things that I do and upholds the same values that I do. I know that I am still figuring out what kind of woman I will be. As I learn more about who I am, I pray that I find my value in who You say I am and that I actually desire to date someone who passionately loves Jesus.

In Jesus' Name, Amen.

Day Five

PRAY FOR A "TIGGER" IN YOUR LIFE

Read: *RALIW* Chapter 4, pages 89-91 (Read the *Pray for a "Tigger" in Your Daughter's Life* section.)

Be aware of the friends you surround yourself with. Parents teach virtue, but friends enhance or tarnish virtue.

DAILY REFLECTION QUESTIONS

1. Do you have a friend, peer, or slightly older mentor in your life who is encouraging you spiritually? If so, who? If not, this is a relationship you want to start praying for. (Like "Tigger" was for my daughter, Jessi.)

____

____

____

____

2. Why is it important for you to pay attention to the friends you surround yourself with? Are your friends positive influences on your life? Do they build you up? Do they encourage you spiritually?

____

____

3. What do you see modeled in your mother's life with the friends and company she keeps? Do you see her with people who propel her closer to God, or do you see her socializing with women who are spiritually mediocre and do not encourage her walk with Jesus?

DAILY PRAYER

Lord, thank You for what You are doing in my life! I ask that You would continue to bring me friends who build me up spiritually and strengthen my faith. I pray You would surround me with people who are truly on fire for Jesus; He is their passion and desire! Real people who pursue a real God. Not religious people, Lord. Not those who say they love Jesus but don't actually follow Him. Lord, my prayer is that You alone would be why I have joy in my life. May the friends in my life push me toward finding happiness in You!

In Jesus' Name, Amen.

VIRTUES CHECKLIST

(Not exhaustive, but a good start!)

a. Courage (see Josh. 1:6-8)

b. Honesty (see Isa. 33:15; Ps.15:2)

c. Respect (see Prov. 9:10; Eph. 6:5-9)

d. Generosity (see Prov. 11:24)

e. Compassion (see Eph. 4:32; 1 Pet. 3:8)

f. Patience (see Ps. 37:7-9)

g. Perseverance (see Rom. 5:3-5)

h. Loyalty (see Prov. 17:17)

i. Forgiveness (see Matt. 18:21-22)

Together

MOTHER/DAUGHTER SESSION

INSTRUCTIONS

You have both gone through Week 5 in the workbook (which covered Chapter 4 in the book). The focus of this week was virtue. Here are some of the questions you can discuss during your mother-daughter session:

- What does the word "virtue" mean to you?
- How does what you wear and how you present yourself communicate virtue?
- In what ways does virtue attract the right guys? (Remember how Ruth attracted Boaz through her virtue? He was the right guy.)
- How has the concept of "modesty" been explained or portrayed to you? What do you think of when you think of someone who is "modest"?
- What does it mean to be a temple of the Holy Spirit, and how should this impact the way we present ourselves (see 1 Cor. 6:19-20)?
- How can you pursue modesty instead of just tolerate it as the "Christian thing to do"? (It's amazing the knock that modesty has taken in the media, especially because

of the outspoken Christians who have endeavored to uphold morality and godly values.)

- Why is it so important to date other believers?
- What does the following statement mean? "The guys you date reveal your spiritual depth." How does that work?
- Missionary dating—what does this mean to you, and why is it a terrible idea that sets us up for disappointment?
- Do you have spiritual mentors in your life? If so, who are they and how has their influence been a help to you and your relationship with God?

It is so important for us to have the right people in our lives, encouraging us to press on toward all of the things God has in store for us. Virtue is fueled by the virtuous influencers in our lives. Do your friends build you up spiritually? Do you have crazy faith friends like the guy in Mark 2, whose friends were so full of faith and trust in Jesus that they lowered the paralyzed guy down through the roof? Talk about faith-*full* friends!

Week 6

BECOMING A YOUNG LADY OF DEVOTION

Becoming a Young Lady of Devotion who seeks to know God's heart is the very best investment you can make to ensure that you will safely attract a man who also has a connection with God's heart.

Day One

RELENTLESS DEVOTION TO JESUS

Read: *RALIW* Chapter 5, pages 93-95 (Read *Ruth's Devotion* and *Modeling Hope or Hopelessness* sections.)

Our devotion to God is primarily about our relationship with Him, and certainly our passion for Him, but those we love are watching that devotion as it ebbs and flows through our lives each day.

DAILY REFLECTION QUESTIONS

1. How does your view of God determine your level of devotion to Him? For example, if you believe God is "cold and exacting," angry, and constantly upset, how will you respond to Him? How will you respond differently if you see Him as a loving Father who offers an unending flow of grace, mercy, and acceptance?

2. How do you usually respond to God in the midst of a trial, circumstance, or challenge? What does this reveal about your devotion?

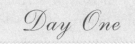

(This is not intended to make you feel bad, but rather to strengthen your devotion if it tends to wane in the midst of difficulty!)

3. Why is it important for your devotion to be constant? What does this say about your relationship with the Lord?

DAILY PRAYER

Lord, help me have hope and show others that they can hope too. If I tend to be more hopeless and negative, fill me with Your joy. If my relationship with You changes and shifts based on whether or not something bad is happening in my life or the situation I am dealing with, take me to the next level of maturity. I pray that I become a woman of constant devotion to Jesus.

In Jesus' Name, Amen.

Day Two

YOUR HOME, YOUR MISSION FIELD

Read: *RALIW* Chapter 5, pages: 95-98 (Read *Unfathomable Impact of a Devoted Mom* and *Mission Fields at the Front Door* sections.)

You and I will someday give an accounting for the spiritual influence we had on everyone who came into our lives.

DAILY REFLECTION QUESTIONS

1. In what ways are you a spiritual influence at home? Do you share your commitment to Jesus with others in your family?

2. How does your father's devotion to Jesus encourage the family's spiritual growth?

3. Are there friends you have right now whom the Lord is encouraging you to be especially loving and kind to? If so, what are some ways you can go above and beyond in their lives by opening up your home to them?

____

____

____

____

Daily Prayer

Lord, I pray that I take this assignment seriously. As people come into my home, help me to take special time to bring Your love, encouragement, a willingness to listen, and whatever else they need into their lives.

In Jesus' Name, Amen.

Day Three

THE PRAYER INVESTMENT

Read: *RALIW* Chapter 5, pages 98-101 (Read *Prayer Requests in a Photo Album* section.)

Friends can be the best kind of cheerleaders for each others' spiritual growth, but they can also tease and undermine each others' spiritual lives. Devotion to Jesus has a differentiating impact on whether or not we will be Bozo magnets or Boaz magnets.

DAILY REFLECTION QUESTIONS

1. What ways do you pray for your friends? If this is something you have not started doing yet, what ways can you start praying for your friends? (These are some of the people you are around most, who influence you the strongest. If you are praying for them, you are helping to spiritually direct the course of their lives and positioning your friends for salvation and increased devotion to Jesus).

2. Can you name at least one of your girlfriends with whom you feel comfortable talking about spiritual things? Do your girlfriends show spiritual growth that you can see, or is it talk only?

3. How do you and your friends talk about the Lord?

DAILY PRAYER

Lord, thank You for prayer. Remind me all the time to pray for my friends. Help me to talk to You about each one of them and pray Your perfect plan for their lives. Above all, I pray that Jesus would be their focus—that they would follow after Him and Him alone.

In Jesus' Name, Amen.

Day Four

DELIVER US FROM THE KINGDOM OF SELF

Read: *RALIW* Chapter 5, pages 101-105 (Read *Deliver Us From the Kingdom of Self, Rescue Me from Me,* and *Mom: The Original Drug Dealer.*)

Me-centric living is in the heart of every man and woman, boy and girl; but it is either enhanced or diminished by those who love them.

DAILY REFLECTION QUESTIONS

1. How is "self" one of your greatest enemies as a believer? In what ways is "self" glorified in the world, negatively influencing the next generation through culture, media, entertainment, et cetera?

____

____

____

2. What does the phrase, "Rescue Me *from* Me" mean to you? How can you rescue yourself from living a "me-centered" lifestyle? What are some ways you can show others it is not *all about you*?

____

____

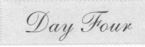

3. Why is it absolutely important for you listen when your mother says *no* to you? How will this help you when you begin dating and someone tries to cross your boundaries?

DAILY PRAYER

Father, deliver me from the trap of self-centeredness. I know it messes with all of us. Show me areas in my life where I am addicted to self, attention, and praise. Thank You, Holy Spirit, for helping me overcome selfishness. Even though I am stuck with self as long as I live, I am also filled with Your Spirit every day I am alive. He alone gives me power over self and helps me to focus on Jesus.

In a world that is becoming more and more self-centered, help me to keep my eyes fixed on Jesus. I pray that I am captivated by His beauty and glory, so much so that the temptation to be distracted by self-centeredness is not even interesting to me!

In Jesus' Name, Amen.

Day Five

TWO ENEMIES: ENTITLEMENT AND GLORY ROBBERS

Read: *RALIW* Chapter 5, pages 105-108 (Read *Entitlement Trumps Gratitude* and *Glory Robber Versus the Lady of Devotion* sections.)

The Young Lady of Devotion knows how to bring glory to God and not rob Him of such glory! May we, by God's grace, become women who are not "ovation-aholics" but God-glorifying Young Ladies of Devotion.

DAILY REFLECTION QUESTIONS

1. What does it look like to be a "glory robber"? How does this work itself out practically in our everyday lives?

____

____

____

2. Do you spend more time focusing on me-centric things (everything is all about *me*), or do you express genuine passion for Jesus, concern for others, and a desire to move past the popularity of being

me-centered? What are some of the tell-tale signs of either one (being me-focused or God/other-focused)?

3. Would you describe yourself as a young lady devoted to Jesus or more of a people-pleasing "ovation-aholic"? (Be honest. Again, God reveals things that He wants to transform and heal!)

DAILY PRAYER

Father, may Your glory be my number one goal. There are so many opportunities for me to take credit for something or to go after recognition or seek attention when the most important thing in my life is giving You the credit that is due to You. Without You, I am nothing and can do nothing.

I want this to be my attitude in life. Help me to be a woman devoted to Jesus. I don't want to ever look for ovation that would deprive me of the wonderful opportunity to give Jesus all of the attention!

In Jesus' Name, Amen.

Together

MOTHER/DAUGHTER SESSION

You have both gone through Week 6 in the workbook (which covered Chapter 5 in the book). The focus of this week was devotion. Here are some of the questions you can discuss during your mother-daughter session:

- Why is it so important to keep constant in our relationship with God? How does this reveal true devotion to Him?
- What does our relationship with God project to the people watching us? (In other words, what does it reveal about our devotion to Him when we are up one day, down the next, and all over the place the rest of the time?)
- Who are some people that you can think of who model steadfast devotion to Jesus?
- Why is it so important to wait for a man who is a spiritual leader—completely devoted to Jesus, not simply wearing the Christian name badge?
- Who are some people you could be praying for (friends)?
- What kinds of conversations do you have about God with your friends? Are they edifying and faith-building?
- What does it mean to be "set free from self"? How is "self" a major enemy when it comes to our devotion to God?

- How is saying "No" actually a good thing?
- What does an "ovation-aholic" look like?

God is not looking for or expecting perfection from you. This is why He gave us Jesus! However, even though we do miss it, blow it, and make mistakes, in the midst of it all we can be wholly devoted to Jesus. Even in our sin, how we respond reveals our devotion to our Master. The world needs to see Christians who are serious. Not wishy-washy. Not all over the place. Devotion is revealed by steadfast commitment. These are the types of people a lady of devotion should surround herself with, from the friends you spend time with, to the guys you date. Ask yourself: Are they pushing you toward steadfast commitment to Jesus, or are they encouraging you to compromise?

Week 7

BECOMING A YOUNG LADY OF PURITY

A woman's purity is, in fact, a lifelong guard of her heart.

Day One

BEING A LADY IN WAITING... IN A SEX-SATURATED WORLD

Read: *RALIW* Chapter 6, pages 109-111 (Read *Ruth's Purity* and *Sex-Saturated Society* sections.)

Just as Ruth's purity allowed her to go to Boaz, request that he function as her kinsman redeemer, and exit his presence as pure as she entered, we can sustain purity even in a context that greatly challenges our commitment to purity.

DAILY REFLECTION QUESTIONS

1. Why do you think there is this idea that it is *impossible* to raise pure girls in a sex-saturated society? Why does it seem like such an impossible task?

___

___

___

2. What are some of the obstacles that you deal with in pursuing and keeping your purity in a sex-saturated culture?

___

3. How does purity guard your heart?

DAILY PRAYER

Father, I know the world is filled with impurity. TV, music, movies, and more are absolutely obsessed with it. Even though it seems impossible to be a lady in waiting who is pure, I believe that by Your grace, and using Your wisdom, it is possible.

In fact, Lord, I ask You to teach me to be one who shines Your light with all this darkness around me. I pray that my life shows others the benefits of going after purity. Not because mom says to, or a pastor tells me to, or because I feel "guilted" into it. I pray I would be one who learns to be pure because I ***desire*** *purity. I want it. Show me the blessing that purity plays in actually protecting and guarding my heart.*

In Jesus' Name, Amen.

Day Two

THE PRINCIPLE OF DIMINISHING RETURNS

Read: *RALIW* Chapter 6, pages 111-114 (Read *MPDP* = *Mandatory Pre-Dating Prep, The Law of Diminishing Returns,* and *The Law of Diminishing Returns: Sexual Brinkmanship* sections)

God made the human body sexually for a particular progression—one that is meant to be followed to its end in the context of marriage. So that very chemistry He wired us with is designed to yearn for more.

DAILY REFLECTION QUESTIONS

1. After reading this section, write out your understanding of what the *Law of Diminishing Returns* is:

____

____

____

____

2. When you read the *Natural Progression Toward Sexual Sin* section on page 112, are there parts of it that seem surprising to you?

____

____

3. Why is it so important to set up strong physical boundaries (so that the *Natural Progression Toward Sexual Sin* you read about does not take place in your life)?

Daily Prayer

Father, help me set up strong, smart boundaries in my life. As I go through this study, I pray I would understand that my body is really Yours and that it is both deserving and demanding of the greatest respect. Show me that, even though everyone else may be "doing it," compromise and going "too far" actually make me less likable in the sight of the guys I like.

Again, Lord, I pray that You would show me the specialness You place on me. As I understand my identity and worth, I will reject anything or anyone who would try to get me to go down a path of impurity.

In Jesus' Name, Amen.

Day Three

ALWAYS PUSHING THE LIMITS

Read: *RALIW* Chapter 6, pages 114-119 (Read *Striving for the Chemistry High, Quicker Sexual Brink in the Next Relationship, Drawing the Line: Remember the No Zone,* and *Why Do Christian Kids Go Too Far?* Sections.)

What you don't know is that with physical touch you are always progressing toward a more potent physical thrill.

DAILY REFLECTION QUESTIONS

1. How does one physical touch progress toward an even stronger physical thrill (if there are no clear boundaries preventing this progression)?

2. How does going to the "No Zone" set the stage for sex?

3. How do you see yourself discussing these principles with your mother and listening to her instruction on some of these more uncomfortable topics? Does the idea of sharing these things with your mother make you feel embarrassed? If so, think about the options: Would you rather experience brief embarrassment or make decisions that could have disastrous effects on your life and future?

___

___

___

___

DAILY PRAYER

Lord, give me the courage to talk about this stuff with my mother. Help me not to feel like she is preaching to me or lecturing me or coming off as some "know it all." Help me to see that she really wants the best for me. Even if it feels embarrassing and uncomfortable—I don't care.

Holy Spirit, give me the strength to move past how I feel in those kinds of conversations so that I can truly learn from this. I know the payoff is worth it!

In Jesus' Name, Amen.

Day Four

THE COST OF GOING TOO FAR

Read: *RALIW* Chapter 6, pages 119-122 (Read *Sex Ruins a Good Relationship*, *Treat Your Girlfriend as a Younger Sister*, and *Additional Encouragement to Wait* sections.)

The painful reality is that most young people grow up hearing that sex before marriage is not God's design without ever hearing about the high price of premarital sex.

DAILY REFLECTION QUESTIONS

1. How does sex ruin a good relationship *or* create a bad one? Have you seen this happen in any of your friends? In other people you may know? What have been some of the results of premarital sex in their relationships?

2. Read First Timothy 5:2. How can you explain this concept of "treating a girlfriend like your sister" as something that is not *gross*, but instead something that will honor you and treat you with the respect that you deserve?

3. Based on the list provided on page 121, what are some of the consequences of premarital sex (beyond just the damage it does to a relationship)? These are the consequences you need to avoid by pursuing purity.

DAILY PRAYER

Lord, protect me from the consequences of premarital sex by helping me pursue purity. I am praying again, Lord, that I would go after purity because I want to. If I spend my time simply trying to resist having sex or going "too far" in my own strength, I will most likely fail. It will become overwhelming.

Give me the strength to really become passionate about purity because of what it will do for my life and my relationship with You. Thanks for helping me avoid Bozos and all the sexual expectations they bring with them.

In Jesus' Name, Amen.

Day Five

NEVER TOO YOUNG...

Read: *RALIW* Chapter 6, pages 122-125 (Read *Never Too Young to Learn About Waiting, Judging Promiscuous Girls Prematurely Robbed of Purity,* and *21st Century Sodom and Gomorrah* sections.)

The driving reason I write books like this and speak to and with thousands of women each year is to encourage, exhort, and beg all of us in the Body of Christ to heed this particular call from God to come out and be separate.

DAILY REFLECTION QUESTIONS

1. How did you respond to the story of Nancy Claire and her Valentine's gift from the little boy? Why do you think it was important to focus on appropriateness instead of sentimentality? Regardless of your current feelings on the story, in the context of purity, how was Nancy set up for success down the road?

____

____

____

____

2. Why is it very important to learn your value—when you are still *very young*?

3. What are some of the factors that make a girl promiscuous? How does God want us to respond to girls who have been caught in this trap? Are any of your friends in this place now? If so, *don't judge them*; instead, *pray* for them! Write their names down on your prayer list or in this workbook and pray.

DAILY PRAYER

Lord, I see that this world is full of impurity. Instead of focusing on the problems and judging the people, help me to be part of bringing solutions. For every problem I experience, for every promiscuous girl I see at school, I will bring them to You in prayer. You are the solution, Jesus. Focusing on the problem makes it easy for me to judge. Help me to pray for these girls' lives to be changed. And Lord, help me to become a young lady of purity who is also part of being the solution in my generation.

In Jesus' Name, Amen.

Together

MOTHER/DAUGHTER SESSION

INSTRUCTIONS

You have both gone through Week 7 in the workbook (which covered Chapter 6 in the book). The focus of this week was purity. Here are some of the questions you can discuss during your mother-daughter session:

- Why do people think that pursuing purity is impossible in our culture?
- What are some of the obstacles we face daily that try to discourage us from pursuing and maintaining our purity?
- The Law of Diminishing Returns—what does this mean to you, and what did you think about it?
- Did the process seem surprising? Extreme? Or right on target?
- Why is it so important to establish clear boundaries before getting into a dating situation?
- How does what you do with your body expose how you perceive your value?
- Do you feel comfortable talking about the kind of stuff you read in this chapter, or is it embarrassing? If so,

why do you feel like it is embarrassing? (To talk about it and to listen to it?)

- How have you been exposed to purity in the past? (Was it presented in a condemning way? Was it simply a "Don't have sex until you're married" lecture? Who did you hear share about it and how did it impact you?)
- How does becoming physical with a guy either destroy a good relationship or prolong a bad one?
- What did you think of the Nancy Claire Valentine's Day story? Was Mom being too extreme, or do you see the value she was communicating to her daughter?
- Why is it so important to pursue purity from a young age?
- How does your relationship with God encourage you to pursue a lifestyle of purity?

It begins with God and ends with purity. You have well-meaning people telling kids not to cross the line *every single day*. Result? They continue to reject purity. Purity is the result of everything we have read thus far. When we are devoted to Jesus and see the value *He* places on us, impurity doesn't even feel like an option any more.

Week 8

Becoming a Young Lady of Security

*W*hatever people say about me...I lay the comments alongside Jesus' biographical sketch of me, because that is where I live, rest, and have confidence.

Day One

MOM: THE MODEL OF SECURITY

Read: *RALIW* Chapter 7, pages 127-129 (Read *Ruth's Security* and *Daughters Reflect Your Security and Insecurities* sections.)

Growing up, the most obvious model a daughter has is her mother. Moms can model the security they find in the Lord, as Ruth certainly did. We can also model "finding" insecurity in all kinds of things.

DAILY REFLECTION QUESTIONS

1. How do you deal with insecurity? Have you tried to take your insecurities to God and rest in Him, or do you try to deal with them by yourself?

2. In what ways are you secure or insecure? How do you deal with worry? Self-image? Confidence?

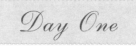

3. Reflect on *your* childhood. How have your past insecurities/securities affected who you are today?

DAILY PRAYER

Lord, show me how to find my security in You because I am Yours. Show me the insecurities that I have and continue to deal with. Reveal them so I can work through my issues and heal from them. Show me areas where my trust is not in You but in shakable, unstable things.

Help me to place my complete trust in You—in Your love, in Your Word, in Your promises, and in Your plan. You will never let me down!

In Jesus' Name, Amen.

Day Two

THE LOVE TANK DEFICIT

Read: *RALIW* Chapter 7, pages 129-133
(Read *Insecurity and a Love Tank Deficit* and
Oh God, Keep an Eye on Her sections.)

Growing in your understanding of the love of God as Father will help fill your love tank. This is important, because love tank deficits are readily exploited by the enemy.

DAILY REFLECTION QUESTIONS

1. What does the "Love Tank" concept mean to you? Specifically, what does a low amount of it in this area produce in you?

2. What are some factors that can contribute to a low "Love Tank" for you?

3. Read John 17:11. How does the fact that *Jesus* Himself prayed for you bring you comfort? How does this encourage you as you pray for protection?

DAILY PRAYER

Father, I come before You today with two specific prayers:

One—I ask You to fill my love tank. I want to be satisfied in Christ and Him alone. May Jesus be my Rock and source of security for the rest of my life.

Two—I come into agreement with the prayer of Jesus in John 17:11. Thank You for releasing protection over my life and for preserving my purity.

In Jesus' Name, Amen.

Day Three

OVERCOMING THE ENEMY'S LIES

Read: *RALIW* Chapter 7, pages 132-136 (Read *Screaming the Truth* and *With God, Who Could Be Against Her* sections.)

The father of lies screams lies at our hearts daily. We can only scream back if our hearts are wallpapered with the truth.

DAILY REFLECTION QUESTIONS

1. What does it look like to "scream back" at the enemy in response to his lies?

2. The ability to "scream back" at the enemy and overcome his lies has everything to do with knowing *the truth*. Re-read the list I provided on pages 133-134. Which of these truths do you struggle with?

3. Why is being confident in the love of God and the love of your family so important for you? How can increasing your security in these areas protect you from sexual sin?

____

____

____

____

Daily Prayer

Father, increase my confidence in Your love and in the love of my family. I pray the love and acceptance I receive from You and from my family will help me to make the right choices.

Protect me from people and places that would try to influence me negatively. Even though I cannot totally avoid them, I pray that I would reject anything that would push me to compromise my purity for security and acceptance.

In Jesus' Name, Amen.

Day Four

READY TO DATE YET?

Read: *RALIW* Chapter 7, pages 136-139 (Read *Timeline for Dating* and *The Gift of No* sections.)

If you cannot say, "no" without worrying about what you friends think—over a movie or music or certain activities—then you are not ready to date. The ability to say, "no" is inextricably linked, not only to your virtue, but to your security.

DAILY REFLECTION QUESTIONS

1. What are some attributes that would make a girl *not ready* to date yet? How does your security and self-confidence factor into finding an appropriate timeline for dating?

2. How does being able to say "no" in small things impact whether or not you are able to date?

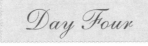

3. Why does insecurity attract older, predatory guys? Why does getting attention from older guys interest younger girls? Why is this a *major problem*?

DAILY PRAYER

Lord, strengthen me to say no. I pray that I am quick to say it because of what I get at home. I will say "no" because I want to make sure I will always be able to enjoy life to the fullest. I pray I would always understand that my "no" and the boundaries I set for myself are to protect me from bad situations—situations I may not fully understand. Boundaries are designed to work with You, Lord, and set me on a course toward the life You have designed for me.

Just like Your commandments are not burdens but are for our good, I pray You would reveal to me how saying "no" protects me from potentially ruining my life. I will boldly say "no" to compromise, insecurity, and making bad decisions.

In Jesus' Name, Amen.

Day Five

Dealing with Bullies, Mean Girls, and Bozo Boys

Read: *RALIW* Chapter 7, pages 139-143 (Read *Source of Insecurity for All Teen Girls, Secure Enough to Face Bullies and Mean Girls*, and *Forgiving Bozo Guys and Mean Girls* sections.)

Prayer can do what God can do. And it will help you see God as your defender—with the co-defender of an attentive mother!

Daily Reflection Questions

1. Review the list on pages 139-140 (or you can flip to pages 133-134 in this workbook). How many of these things are a struggle for you?

2. In what ways have you dealt with bullying or *mean girls*? How did you handle these issues?

3. What are some appropriate ways for you to deal with bullying, mean girls, or mocking Bozo boys? (Remember my letter to Kristi about Nancy Claire.)

DAILY PRAYER

Father, show me how to pray for the bullies and mean girls who are in my life (or were in my life in the past).

People like this are always going to be around. When I do have to deal with bullies or mean girls, show me how to give these people to You in prayer.

In Jesus' Name, Amen.

COMMON WORRIES FOR TEEN GIRLS

Here is a list that was the result of interviews with teen girls age twelve to fifteen. The girls were asked to share the things they worried about. This list is a reminder for all moms to pray for the development of a Young Lady of Security.

- Girls talking about me
- What other people think about whatever I'm doing
- If my friends are really going to be my friends around other people
- If I get in a fight with my friends, are we going to hate each other and become rivals?
- Spiders
- Grades
- Boys
- Friend situation (who is being mean)
- Rumors
- Succeeding in school and in general
- Trying to be good at everything
- Trying to make myself worth someone's time

- Fighting with siblings
- Loneliness
- Screwing up my life and not realizing it
- That people will think I'm weird
- Not making the right choices
- Gaining weight
- If people judge me from my appearance
- That I won't know how to get out of a bad situation
- Getting into trouble

Together

MOTHER/DAUGHTER SESSION

INSTRUCTIONS

You have both gone through Week 8 in the workbook (which covered Chapter 7 in the book). The focus of this week was security. Here are some of the questions you can discuss during your mother-daughter session:

- What are some ways people deal with insecurity?
- How do you deal with insecurity?
- What is our "love tank" and why is it so important to keep it full?
- What are some ways to keep this "love tank" full?
- Why is it important that we learn to "scream back" at the enemy? What does this mean to you?
- What are some of lies that the enemy tells you that cause you to become insecure? (These are the very things you need to "scream back" at.)
- Why is it is important for us to know the truth in order to deal with the lies of the enemy?
- Explain some of the factors that you think make a girl ready to start dating?
- How comfortable are you saying "No"?

- How is it a problem when older guys express interest in younger girls?
- What are some ways to handle bullying or "mean girls"?

I know it may seem a bit strange at first to "scream back" at the enemy. Of course, I'm not always meaning that you are supposed to yell at the top of your lungs at him. (Although there is a time and a place!)

The reality is that insecurity is the result of believing his lies. When we worry. When we question our value in God's sight. When we stumble over who we are or who we're not. When we think that having a boyfriend or getting in *that* relationship with *that* person will mean that "we've arrived"—we have fallen into the trap. This is where we need to scream, ladies. Our security is in Christ alone. He has given us value. The cross reveals the beyond-expensive value He has placed on us.

Week 9

Becoming a Young Lady of Contentment

Such an assignment is not given to cause suffering, but to prevent it. Women experience so much needless pain when they run ahead of God's format.

Day One

DISCONTENTMENT THAT SUFFOCATES JOY

Read: *RALIW* Chapter 8, pages 149-151 (Read *Ruth's Contentment* and *Discontentment Suffocates Joy* sections.)

When we find ourselves discontented, we are all too often focusing on what is missing from our lives rather than seeing what is going well with them.

DAILY REFLECTION QUESTIONS

1. How does being *boyfriend-less* produce discontentment in many girls? Why do you think this is such a big issue? (What factors make girls think that being in a relationship is being content?)

2. In what ways does comparison create discontentment and ultimately steal our joy? How do you personally deal with comparison and discontentment?

3. How is self-pity *inverted* pride? What does it mean to have an "over-inflated view of what one deserves"?

Daily Prayer

Father, thanks for all of the blessings You have given me. They are too many to count. I pray that instead of being caught up in comparison or discontentment, I would spend my time being thankful. Even when I deal with the temptation to be discontented, give me the strength to lift my eyes and focus on who You are, what You've done, and what You are doing.

Make my spirit of thanksgiving and gratitude unmistakable to others. I want my attitude to be a weapon against the comparison, discontentment, and self-pity that is so popular around me.

In Jesus' Name, Amen.

Day Two

SERVING OTHERS AND SILENCING THE WHINING

Read: *RALIW* Chapter 8, pages 151-157 (Read *Contentment and Holy Sweat, Contentment and Boredom,* and *Limit Self-Indulgent Emotionalism* sections.)

Learning contentment does not mean expecting changes in our circumstances, but expecting Jesus to be enough in our circumstances.

DAILY REFLECTION QUESTIONS

1. How does serving others (being a Young Lady of Diligence) develop you into being a Young Lady of Contentment? How is serving other people a "perfect escort out of self-pity" and something that enhances contentment?

___

___

___

2. In what ways can you serve others (as an alternative to being bored)? Start with this: What are some specific ways you have demonstrated service toward others in the past? What areas are you passionate about? Use your talents to be a blessing to someone else!

3. How does whining and self-centeredness actually set girls up to attract Bozo guys? Evaluate yourself. Are you content, or are you frequently whining? Evaluate the influences in your life: Who might be whining and bringing you along on their bandwagon?

DAILY PRAYER

Father, I want be content. If there are areas in my life where I am discontent or whining, help me stop it immediately and remember the things You have blessed me with. I freely accept Your incredible grace to do what I cannot do in my own strength.

In Jesus' Name, Amen.

Day Three

DEALING WITH UNREALISTIC EXPECTATIONS

Read: *RALIW* Chapter 8, pages 157-160 (Read *Discontentment and Loneliness, Contentment and Unrealistic Expectations,* and *Want a "Ten" But Keep Getting a "Five"* sections.)

When you have a dateless Friday night or even a "friendship dateless" one, it is a tutorial in contentment through the strength of Jesus.

DAILY REFLECTION QUESTIONS

1. How can we embrace loneliness as God's will *for right now* and accept it as a positive thing?

2. How can you use disappointing situations and circumstances as teachable moments in your life?

3. What is your understanding of the "Ten Versus Five Theory"? How can applying this perspective save you from experiencing disappointment and being constantly let down because of unrealistic expectations?

DAILY PRAYER

Lord, I want to do only what You have already planned for me. I can't do it all, and I am not expected to! I understand that many people have expectations that they place on me. I also place expectations on myself. Help me figure out what is most important so I can take care of those things and fulfill those responsibilities.

In Jesus' Name, Amen.

Day Four

SOME KEYS TO DEFEATING DISCONTENTMENT

Read: *RALIW* Chapter 8, pages 161-165 (Read *Discontentment Blinds Us, Boy Craziness: A Common Assault on Contentment,* and *Cheering on Discontentment* sections.)

Contentment does not flow from finally getting the approval of others. Contentment flows from knowing one has already been approved by the King of kings!

DAILY REFLECTION QUESTIONS

1. What are some areas in your life where you are dealing with jealousy toward those who have what you have always wanted? (These are your "Rachels.") How does jealousy actually enhance your discontentment and blind you to God's blessing in your life?

2. How does "boy-craziness" rob girls of contentment?

____

____

3. In what ways do friends and peers actually *encourage* discontentment in our lives? How have you experienced this in the past (or present)?

____

____

____

____

DAILY PRAYER

Father, remind me that I am special and valuable just because I am Yours. My value does not come from what people think of me. Show me where I have jealousy in my heart. I am going to be honest and tell You the ways I have been jealous now. I promise to receive Your forgiveness. (Take this time to search your heart and confess any jealousy to the Lord.)

Lord, show me how to grow up to be a person who is not moved by what others have. I pray that I would be so content with myself, and in the assignment You have for me, that nothing would distract me and pull me off-course.

In Jesus' Name, Amen.

List of the Top Ten Ways to Bust Boy-Craziness

1. Write love letters to God.
2. Create a list of great movies and books that don't fuel impure thoughts and romance.
3. Hang out with friends who aren't boy-crazy.
4. Invest time in the "man in your life"—your dad.
5. Exercise or get involved in sports.
6. Get a mentor to talk to about it.
7. Write a list of your future husband's qualities.
8. Begin a journal to your future husband.
9. Read *Passion and Purity* and *Lady in Waiting*.
10. Go on a mission trip.

Day Five

STARVING DISCONTENTMENT AND FINDING A BIBLICAL MODEL

Read: *RALIW* Chapter 8, pages 165-168 (Read *"Don't Waste Brain Cells, Child," Don't Feed Discontentment Through Toxic Giving*, and *Ruth, the Proverbs 31 Woman*, and *Contentment* sections.)

The next time you get a "no," just remember the propensity to "toxic giving" and how it can ultimately poison you with discontentment.

DAILY REFLECTION QUESTIONS

1. What are some things in your life that help you "bust discontentment" (just like Ella's discontentment-buster list on pages 165-166)?

2. How can we feed discontentment through "toxic giving"? What does this look like and how does it create an attitude of entitlement?

3. Think about creative ways you could use Ruth and Proverbs 31. Why are these portions of Scripture so important in growing up to be content?

Daily Prayer

Lord, help me to avoid discontentment in every way that I can. Let me starve it by not giving in to "toxic giving." Give me wisdom to avoid thinking I am owed things.

Finally, show me how to live out what I read in the Bible. Give me wisdom to learn, but above all, the grace to live it so what I learn helps me grow closer to You.

In Jesus' Name, Amen.

Ella's Discontentment-Buster List

(from pages 165-166)

- Never allow yourself to complain about anything—not even the weather.
- Never picture yourself in any other circumstances or someplace else.
- Never compare your lot with another's. (See Psalms 16.)
- Never allow yourself to wish this or that had been otherwise.
- Never dwell on tomorrow—remember that (tomorrow) is God's, not ours.

Parallels Between the Proverbs 31 Woman and Ruth

I encourage you to find a way to use the following Scriptures as tools for a Bible study with your mother.

Perhaps over the course of eight weeks, as a group you can go through each of these characteristics, with each week being a different characteristic. Have your daughter/the girls look up these verses in their Bibles and talk about what they mean, how they apply today, and some ways they could incorporate them into their own lives.

1. Devoted to her family (see Ruth 1:15-18; Prov. 31:10-12,23)
2. Delighted in her work (see Ruth 2:2; Prov. 31:13)
3. Diligent in her labor (see Ruth 2:7,17,23; Prov. 31:14-22,24,27)
4. Dedicated to godly speech (see Ruth 2:10,13; Prov. 31:26)
5. Dependent on God (see Ruth 2:12; Prov. 31:30)
6. Dressed with care (see Ruth 3:3; Prov. 31:22,25)
7. Discreet with men (see Ruth 3:6-13; Prov. 31:11-12,23)
8. Delivered blessings (Ruth 4:14-15; Prov. 31:28-29,31)

Together

MOTHER/DAUGHTER SESSION

INSTRUCTIONS

You have both gone through Week 9 in the workbook (which covered Chapter 8 in the book). The focus of this week was contentment. Here are some of the questions you can discuss during your mother-daughter session:

- How does being without a boyfriend make many girls discontent?
- In what ways do comparison and jealousy make us discontent with what we already have?
- Why does service to other people help develop contentment? (Especially to those who are less fortunate.)
- How does self-centeredness actually attract Bozo guys?
- What are some of the benefits of being alone?
- Why do you think so many people consider being alone such a bad thing? Do you think this has anything to do with how they understand their value? (Other people assign their value.)
- What does the "Ten Versus Five" theory mean to you?
- In what ways do people set themselves up for disappointment and discontentment through their own expectations?

- List some of the ways that our friends can actually discourage contentment.

- What does it mean to be content in the assignment that God has uniquely given to you?

- Explain the concept of "toxic giving" and how that easily creates discontentment in our lives.

Discontentment sets us up for poor decision-making. Why? We see what others have and either 1) think that is what we *need* when in fact, it is *not at all* or 2) even if it is a positive thing and we could benefit from it, we still become jealous of what they have and become willing to do all sorts of ridiculous things to get it—*now*.

Let's become okay with where we are and what we have *now*. I'm convinced that those who learn how to enjoy their *now* are being set up for an incredible *later*.

Week 10

Becoming a Young Lady of Conviction

It is conviction in the principles of godly standards for dating and marriage that enables us to say "no" when that's required and to say "yes" to God's ways.

Day One

THE STARTING PLACE OF CONVICTION

Read: *RALIW* Chapter 9, pages 171-175
(Read *Ruth's Convictions, A Lady of Clear Convictions,* and *The Stud Purse* sections.)

Once you begin noticing the boys in your world, it is time to develop the standards that define your convictions.

DAILY REFLECTION QUESTIONS

1. What is the "double booked" reality of the heart? How does this relate to the choices that we make daily? Why is it so important that you are aware of this heart condition when it comes to dating?

2. How is developing conviction the *most important* preparation you can make before dating?

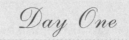

3. Identify some ways you can distinguish between a Bozo and a Boaz (review the list on pages 173-174 if you need to).

DAILY PRAYER

God, help me prepare for dating in the best way possible. Beyond clothes, make-up, hair, and all of those external things, I want to hold to my purity and value in You. This is something only Your Spirit can do, so I pray He would guide me along the way.
While going through this study, I know I have messed up and made mistakes; thanks for grace. Thank You for forgiveness and second chances...and third chances...and that Your grace is always there for me. I will take it. I won't believe the lie of the enemy that says, "You are unworthy to develop convictions when you've already made mistakes." Jesus, You have set me free and I am completely free. I am free to move forward and build strong convictions that will position me for Your best!

In Jesus' Name, Amen.

Comparisons Between a Bozo and a Boaz

(See Second Samuel 13 and Ruth 2.)

1. Bozo is controlled by emotion.

   - Boaz controls his emotions. (He may get upset, but knows what to do with it.)

2. Bozo is angered when he doesn't get his way.

   - Boaz can rise above disappointment; he knows God will give him peace.

3. Bozo doesn't notice the needs of others. (He might turn it on for you, but don't be impressed unless he does the same for the person across the table.)

   - Boaz is courteous and aware, goes the extra mile, and has plenty of room to love lots of people.

4. Bozo is very critical of others and very intolerant.

   - Boaz is tolerant of imperfection because he knows who he is.

5. Bozo is self-centered; he always wants it on his terms (lust thrives in this heart).

   - Boaz is other-centered, and therefore self-controlled (lust is constrained in his heart).

6. Bozo is rigid and his viewpoint is the only conclusion.

    - Boaz is teachable; his heart and mind are open.

7. Bozo always makes excuses for not doing a task well. (If you marry a man like that, you become part of the excuse team.) No one is ever accountable for the way he lives and he always wants sympathy.

    - Boaz strives to do his work to the best of his ability and to the glory of Jesus.

8. Bozo lacks integrity; he has no conscience when exploiting a girl's purity.

    - Boaz has integrity and is kind, merciful, and gentle. These qualities fuel his protection of a girl's purity.

Day Two

CALLED TO BE A STANDARD-SETTER

Read: *RALIW* Chapter 9, pages 175-177 (Read *No Bozo Pajamas* and *Mentored by Hollywood* sections.)

Boys as well as girls are being babysat and even mentored by Hollywood. This is how they are learning about the opposite sex.

DAILY REFLECTION QUESTIONS

1. How is a generation being raised and mentored by Hollywood? What values are being driven into you through the media?

2. What are the benefits to being a young lady of conviction who acts like a princess in God's Kingdom? Specifically—what does such an example reveal to the Bozo guys out there (who are unfortunately increasing in number)?

3. How do your convictions actually set a standard for how boys end up behaving toward you? (This is revealed in how you dress, present yourself, guard your purity, etc.)

DAILY PRAYER

Thank You, Father, for never leaving my side as I become a woman. You have called me to be a standard-setter among my friends, school, and community. Make me aware of how my convictions actually play a part in how boys grow up to be men, too. Help me to see myself as precious in Your eyes and treat myself that way.

I pray that as I always protect my value through the convictions You place on my heart, boys will respect me and protect these things as well.

In Jesus' Name, Amen.

Day Three

ESSENTIAL BOAZ QUALITIES

Read: *RALIW* Chapter 9, pages 177-180 (Read *Most Significant List on an iPhone* section.)

You need to decide in advance what a man worth waiting for is like. You don't decide in the moment when you're crushing on a guy. You decide in advance—before the emotional tsunami hits.

DAILY REFLECTION QUESTIONS

1. What are some advantages to keeping a list of "ideal guy" traits always handy? How does continually focusing on this list actually set you up to reject anyone less than your desired standard?

2. Why is it important for you to create this list *before* you start dating or "crushing on" someone?

3. How do you—as a young lady of conviction—actually remind guys of what they are *supposed* to act like towards girls?

DAILY PRAYER

Lord, help me as I create a list of the essential things I will look for in my ideal guy. I know this doesn't mean he will be perfect. This doesn't mean he will be something out of a fairy tale. We all come with issues and we all are working through stuff. But show me the balance. And Lord, help me to pray for this man. (You might want to pray through the sample list provided on the next page.)

I pray that the he is a man radically committed to Jesus Christ—not in title or name only. I pray that I would pursue one who pursues and relies completely upon You. Help me to create this list as soon as possible.

In Jesus' Name, Amen.

SAMPLE "MR. RIGHT" LIST

1. Spirit-controlled Christian
2. Jesus #1 in his life, not just an ornament
3. Broken: understands how to rely totally upon Jesus
4. Ministry-minded: wherever he is, he is available
5. Motivator: a man of vision, concerned about lost souls
6. Sensitive spirit: in tune to the needs of others
7. Understands the awesome responsibility of a husband to his wife
8. Humble enough to be a disciple (teachable) and able to disciple others
9. Man of prayer: knows the key to success is his private time with God
10. Family man: desires to have children and raise them properly for God's glory

Day Four

APPEARANCES CAN BE DECEIVING

Read: *RALIW* Chapter 9, pages 180-184 (Read *Superficiality of Appearance* section.)

Whenever I hear girls describing guys as being so cute or so hot, I always ask, "What is his heart like? How does he treat those around him?" God's Word speaks loudly to the superficiality of appearance.

DAILY REFLECTION QUESTIONS

1. How can physical appearances be deceiving?

2. Most likely, you have certain physical preferences when it comes to the "ideal guy." How can you be open and flexible on some of the physical stuff to focus on the more important things (namely, those qualities that *should* be on your "ideal guy" list)? If your list is made up of mostly physical characteristics, there is some work that needs to be done!

3. What does the following statement mean: "Guys play at love to have sex?" How is this a warning to you about the selfish, external desires that Bozo guys have when it comes down to sex and getting a girl to go "all the way"?

DAILY PRAYER

Lord, help me to know the value of looking beyond appearances when it comes to dating. I pray that when it comes to those essential things I want in an "ideal guy," I ***always*** *choose a godly character over someone I think is "hot" or "cute." Help me make the best decision for my life, Lord. If I don't already, help me to see that good looks are temporary and can be deceiving. Also show me that You are a good Father. You are the giver of good gifts, and You are not—****not*** *going to disappoint me when it comes to providing me with the ideal guy.*

In Jesus' Name, Amen.

Day Five

CREATING A FIRE WALL OF PRAYER

Read: *RALIW* Chapter 9, pages 184-18
(Read *Fire Wall of Prayer Around Our Girls* section.)

You are around boys at church who are Christians, but they don't live up to their names, either. They are indeed princes related to the King of kings, but they bring dishonor to that name.

DAILY REFLECTION QUESTIONS

1. How can you pray for the guys who show interest in dating you—especially Christian guys who may not be *walking the walk*?

2. What is a pretty reliable way of determining whether a girl has been involved physically with her boyfriend?

____

____

3. List *four* specific things you are going to pray for your dating life on a daily basis.

a. ____________________________________

b. ____________________________________

c. ____________________________________

d. ____________________________________

DAILY PRAYER

Thank You, Lord, for giving me prayer; it is so important to my relationship with You. Even though I feel alone sometimes, Holy Spirit, You are with me every second. As Jesus said, You are with me and You live inside of me.

I pray that You would strengthen my convictions. Wherever I am, I know I can be stronger. We all can be. Lord, may my convictions be strengthened as I pursue a relationship with You above everything else. I pray nothing else this world offers would draw me away from You. Show me the shallowness in all of the competition out there. Show me how lifeless and joyless it all is compared to knowing You.

In Jesus' Name, Amen.

FOR ADDITIONAL STUDY...

Women are well acquainted with the "ideal woman" chapter, Proverbs 31. Very few know about the "ideal man" chapter excerpted verse by verse, below.

Ruth 2:1-16

> 1. *Now Naomi had a relative on her husband's side, from the clan of Elimelech, a man of standing, whose name was Boaz.*
>
> 2. *And Ruth the Moabitess said to Naomi, "Let me go to the fields and pick up the leftover grain behind anyone in whose eyes I find favor." Naomi said to her, "Go ahead, my daughter."*
>
> 3. *So she went out and began to glean in the fields behind the harvesters. As it turned out, she found herself working in a field belonging to Boaz, who was from the clan of Elimelech.*
>
> 4. *Just then Boaz arrived from Bethlehem and greeted the harvesters, "The Lord be with you!" "The Lord bless you!" they called back.*
>
> 5. *Boaz asked the foreman of his harvesters, "Whose young woman is that?"*
>
> 6. *The foreman replied, "She is the Moabitess who came back from Moab with Naomi.*
>
> 7. *"She said, 'Please let me glean and gather among the sheaves behind the harvesters.' She went into the field and has worked steadily from morning till now, except for a short rest in the shelter."*

8. So Boaz said to Ruth, "My daughter, listen to me. Don't go and glean in another field and don't go away from here. Stay here with my servant girls.

9. "Watch the field where the men are harvesting, and follow along after the girls. I have told the men not to touch you. And whenever you are thirsty, go and get a drink from the water jars the men have filled."

10. At this, she bowed down with her face to the ground. She exclaimed, "Why have I found such favor in your eyes that you notice me—a foreigner?"

11. Boaz replied, "I've been told all about what you have done for your mother-in-law since the death of your husband—how you left your father and mother and your homeland and came to live with a people you did not know before.

12. "May the Lord repay you for what you have done. May you be richly rewarded by the Lord, the God of Israel, under whose wings you have come to take refuge."

13. "May I continue to find favor in your eyes, my lord," she said. "You have given me comfort and have spoken kindly to your servant—though I do not have the standing of one of your servant girls."

14. At mealtime Boaz said to her, "Come over here. Have some bread and dip it in the wine vinegar." When she sat down with the harvesters, he offered her some roasted grain. She ate all she wanted and had some left over.

15. As she got up to glean, Boaz gave orders to his men, "Even if she gathers among the sheaves, don't embarrass her.

16. "Rather, pull out some stalks for her from the bundles and leave them for her to pick up, and don't rebuke her."

After studying this chapter, consider reading the contrasting "Bozo" chapter: Second Samuel 13:1-16.

Together

MOTHER/DAUGHTER SESSION

INSTRUCTIONS

You have both gone through Week 10 in the workbook (which covered Chapter 9 in the book). The focus of this week was conviction. Here are some of the questions you can discuss during your mother-daughter session:

- How does clearly defining your convictions prepare you for relationships?
- Discuss the list of characteristics comparing a Boaz and a Bozo.
- In what ways is a generation being raised and mentored by people in Hollywood?
- How does a woman of conviction actually have the ability to set the standards for men in society?
- Explain how creating a list of "ideal guy" traits (and keeping it very handy!) is so important to maintaining your convictions.
- What type of emphasis do people place on physical appearance when it comes to being attracted to someone and dating them? How important is appearance?
- How can physical appearances be deceiving, and ultimately very destructive to a relationship?

Earlier on, we talked about how you cannot change a guy by dating him, thus the insanity of *Missionary Dating*. That said, I believe that as a generation of young women rise up who model deep convictions (one such conviction being the refusal to date someone who does not share her deep convictions), the moral temperature has to change. Bozos will start seeing that their tactics and tricks are failing because a new kind of woman is arising.

I believe the young lady in waiting is part of a movement that will change the way women are viewed entirely. Your convictions don't just protect you, but they are modeling what conviction looks like to the many eyes that are watching.

Week 11

Becoming a Young Lady of Patience

My heart's passion is twofold: for all of God's girls to wait for His best; and for me to be used as His instrument to encourage their waiting, whether it be for a husband and family, a vocation, or any other calling of God.

Day One

ENTERING THE SCHOOL OF PATIENCE

Read: *RALIW* Chapter 10, pages 191-198
(Read *Ruth's Patience, Is "Wait" a Cuss Word,* and
Vulnerability to Missionary Dating sections.)

Postponing present pleasures for future fulfillment is a concept that is familiar to most of us. Yet it is less frequently practiced in our more recent "fast food," "instant access" generations.

DAILY REFLECTION QUESTIONS

1. What can you learn when you *postpone* present pleasures for future fulfillment? How does patience build your character and specifically prepare you for your Boaz?

2. How can you be patient throughout the day?

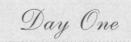

3. Why do you think so many young girls are so negative toward the idea of *waiting* for God's best?

4. How does impatience actually set a girl up to become vulnerable to "missionary dating"?

DAILY PRAYER

Lord, I ask that You show me areas in my life where I am not being patient. I know we all blow it sometimes. But God, I want to live out an attitude of patience. I pray that I practice patience when I am at home, school, and other places so that I can appreciate its importance in my life—especially when it comes to dating. I know there will be plenty of opportunities to practice patience. Remind me that there is no test that I experience that you have not already given me the tools to overcome. Thank You, Lord.

In Jesus' Name, Amen.

DON'T SETTLE

I hope you don't consider me to meddle,
When I say don't settle.
Have you heard my heart scream?
Don't give up your dream.
So many have settled for Prince Harming,
Rather than courageously wait for Prince Charming.
Settling for a Bozo,
Whose heart will be a no show.
Despairing over your absent knight in shining armor,
Will escort you into the arms of a carnival charmer.
Your Designer has dreamed much better for you,
Don't settle for a man who can't love you through and through.

Day Two

MOM: THE SPIRITUAL MONITOR

Read: *RALIW* Chapter 10, pages 198-202
(Read *Enhanced Heartbreak, Help to Emotionally Constrain a Girl's Crushes,* and *Letter from Annie* sections.)

Helping to emotionally constrain our daughters while they grow in patience is an emotional harness that will protect them immeasurably throughout high school and college and thereafter!

DAILY REFLECTION QUESTIONS

1. In what ways can you *constrain* yourself—specifically, in the area of dating and relationships? What does this look like, and what does it protect you from?

____

____

____

____

2. How can you avoiding getting carried away by your "crushes" and the guys you "like"?

____

____

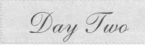

3. What does the following statement mean to you? *"To raise a Lady in Waiting, one must be a Mother in Waiting."*

DAILY PRAYER

Father, help me to be a Lady in Waiting. I know there can be danger in the way I talk about the boys I like, have a crush on, or am dating. Help me to choose my words carefully. I pray that before I speak, You would remind me not to get carried away. Help me to know You sincerely care about me and want to see me make the absolute best decisions in my life. And God, continue to help my heart to want to pursue You in a deeper way. As You become my desire—more and more—I pray that patience becomes more and more natural for me.

In Jesus' Name, Amen.

Day Three

PATIENCE PROTECTS

Read: *RALIW* Chapter 10, pages 202-206 (Read *Missed Out—While Waiting, Protected Not Rejected,* and *Impatient and Aggressive Girls* sections.)

May God allow you to clearly see that your mom is your cheerleader. One of her common cheers is, "Sweetie, you are being protected, not rejected!"

DAILY REFLECTION QUESTIONS

1. What are the things that you *miss out on* when you wait? How can these be a positive thing instead of a negative thing?

2. Why does waiting *protect* you? Why is the lack of attention from boys (particularly the Bozos) *not* rejection but *protection*?

3. What are some factors that drive girls toward being aggressive in their pursuit of relationships?

DAILY PRAYER

Father, show me that waiting protects me and prepares me for the guy You have picked out especially for me. Also, it saves me from the devastating pain experienced by giving my heart away to the wrong person.

Lord Jesus, I ask that You keep my heart safe. Also, help me to see why it is so important to protect myself as Your beautiful treasure and save myself for the man who will also protect me.

In Jesus' Name, Amen.

Day Four

SETTING BOUNDARIES IN ADVANCE

Read: *RALIW* Chapter 10, pages 206-209 (Read *Besides "Sixteen," What Other Dating Prep is Needed?, Who Owns Your Body?,* and *Vulnerable Situations Sexually* sections.)

For any girl, young or not-so-young, the waiting period does not have to be wasted. The waiting for one's first date or one's first love is a time to evaluate your own personal strategy for moral purity.

DAILY REFLECTION QUESTIONS

1. How is the waiting period a time that does not have to be wasted for you? What can you do during this time that will help prepare you for Boaz?

2. Why it is so important that you establish *clear boundaries* before you start dating? How will this protect you for *when* you start dating?

3. What are some ways you can avoid getting wrapped up in sexual situations? (You can review my list on page 208.)

DAILY PRAYER

I ask, Holy Spirit, that You make it clear to me if I am doing anything that might be destructive or am with any person who is not Your plan or purpose for me. I pray You would give me the wisdom and the ability to not go to these places or be with these people. Holy Spirit, make Your will clear to me.

Help me establish solid boundaries now so that when I start dating, I know where I stand and I will not be budged. Give me grace to take stands for purity that might be unpopular with my friends and that are definitely unpopular in this generation. I pray that I don't go after popularity but pursue purity because of who I am in Christ.

In Jesus' Name, Amen.

JACKIE'S PRE-TEMPTATION PROGRAM

Prior to your first date, you should know this list as well as you know your home address. These points are like the markings on your moral compass. Before you go out the door of your home with a young man, you should have these in your heart as pre-temptation preparation.

1. How far would I go if Jesus were sitting next to me? (See Hebrews 4:13.)
2. What would a person I respect think of me? (See 1 Timothy 4:12.)
3. If we break up, can I look the other person in the eye? (See Acts 24:16.)
4. Do I feel guilty? (See Psalms 38:4.)
5. Does it turn me on sexually? (See First Peter 2:11.)
6. Would I want my parents to see what I am doing? (See Colossians 3:20.)
7. Would I want my future mate doing this right now? (See Hebrews 13:4.)

Day Five

WAITING FOR LOVE, REJECTING LUST

Read: *RALIW* Chapter 10, pages 209-212 (Read *Impatience: The Pen Writing Post-Dated Checks for Marital Unfaithfulness, Difference Between Lust and Love,* and *Patiently Waiting: How Will I Know It Is Him?* Sections.)

The patience in your heart will allow you to wait for "true love." True love requires a maturity and commitment that impatience has no tolerance for.

DAILY REFLECTION QUESTIONS

1. How does remaining pure *before* marriage actually set the stage for a relationship that will not be hurt by adultery and unfaithfulness in the future?

____

____

____

____

2. What is your understanding of the differences between *lust* and *love*? How would you define each term? How does lust actually violate the definition of love that Paul provides in First Corinthians 13:4-5?

3. I'm sure you are asking the question: "How will I know it's him?" (referring to the appearance of your Boaz). How do *you* think you will *know* you have met the right guy?

Daily Prayer

Father, keep showing me how to become a Lady in Waiting who actually takes that title seriously. It is not a negative thing to me; instead, it is something I am absolutely proud of and something I refuse to compromise or give up. Continue to show me how valuable I am to You.

I know the day will come when I will meet Your best for my life. Help me to pray for him now, so when the day comes we are both ready. I pray You give me clarity to walk in Your perfect plan now...and for the rest of my life.

In Jesus' Name, Amen.

TRUE LOVE LIST

Based on First Corinthians 13:4-8

- True love distinguishes between a person and a body.
- True love always generates respect.
- True love is self-giving.
- True love can thrive without physical expression.
- True love seeks to build relationship.
- True love embraces responsibility.
- True love can postpone gratification.
- True love is a commitment.

Together

MOTHER/DAUGHTER SESSION

INSTRUCTIONS

You have both gone through Week 11 in the workbook (which covered Chapter 10 in the book). The focus of this week was patience. Here are some of the questions you can discuss during your mother-daughter session:

- Why has "wait" become such a bad word for so many young people?
- How does impatience actually set someone up to start missionary dating?
- What are the dangers of parents getting overly excited about the people their kids are dating? (This is why it is important to be a Mother in Waiting!)
- How can the waiting process actually protect someone from making bad decisions?
- What are some of the factors that cause women to be aggressive in pursuing guys?
- How does sticking to your convictions actually encourage you to be patient?
- In what ways can you avoid a vulnerable situation?

- How does pursuing purity now and waiting for God's best actually set someone up for a marriage that is not as likely to be compromised through adultery?
- What is your understanding of the difference between lust and love? What seems to be the more popular one in culture?
- What are some practical things you can do to help determine whether or not you have met the right guy?

This was your last mother/daughter session for this study. My prayer? That these dates continue long after you finish *Raising a Lady in Waiting*. I did not set this up merely to write a book. I told you, my vision is a movement. It's a lifestyle. It's a culture where mothers and daughters connect and benefit from each other.

I know age separates you, but we need to push past that. Young people need the wisdom and experience from the older (I prefer the term *wiser*) generation, and we—yes, us wiser folks—need the vigor, passion, and energy of the young generation. When we link together, above all, in our family relationships, we literally set ourselves up to become world changers.

Closing Remarks from Jackie

And thus, Week 11 concludes our time together.

On the heels of the last question, let me clarify—the "right guy" is *one* guy. Boaz is a husband, not a boyfriend or crush. Be aware of this! Even after going through this book, you might be absolutely convinced you found Mr. Right. You may think he compliments all of the ideal guy traits on your list. Listen, there may be guys who are right guys, but not *your* right guy. Make sense? This is why it is so important not to jump the gun too soon. (Like writing your first name next to his last name before you're even dating!)

I encourage you, without sounding like I'm begging—enjoy this season of your life. I live and breathe to see a generation of young women actually make the most of the beautiful life God has given them. This is why I'm so "in your face" and honest about what I think about the topics we covered in our time together (I'm sure it didn't take long to figure that out). I want you to take this time and enjoy it for what it is—a season in your life that you will never get back, but it has the potential to shape the course of your future in the most wonderful ways imaginable!

Thanks a bunch for taking this journey with me.

And don't forget—your mom is your number one cheerleader and coach! Your friends aren't. The media can't be. School won't do it sufficiently. Church can't do it completely. It's *Mom!* I started with that reminder and I must end with it. This study is designed to remind you that your mom is actually *for you*. That is what I pray was communicated to you as you went through this study together. Even if you were reluctant or thought it would be lame or whatever. This is sowing seeds into your life that are going to produce major harvest.

My final words of encouragement to you? Refuse to compromise. Say "No." Pursue King Jesus above all. Be open to talk with Mom about this stuff—even the embarrassing parts. Patience is a good thing. But when it comes down to it, trust your future to Jesus. He is so faithful, and I promise He loves you more than you could even imagine. He is ever trustworthy, and truly the greatest example you could set your eyes on! When you and your King are tight, everything else will come into its place.

Running alongside you,

Jackie Kendall

Notes